WORKBOOK

For

What Lights You Up?:

Light Your Path and Take the Next
Major Step in Your Career

Irene Franklin

Table of Contents

HOW TO USE THIS WORKBOOK

Welcome to Mary Olson-Menzel's companion workbook, What Lights You Up?: Illuminate Your Path and Take the Next Big Step in Your Career. This workbook is intended to provide you an organized strategy to engaging fully with the book's material. It promises to help you define your interests, shape your career path, and reclaim your professional power by summarizing major chapters, emphasizing key lessons, presenting self-reflection questions, providing life-changing tasks, and prompting self-evaluation.

This companion workbook is an additional resource designed to improve your experience with What Lights You Up? It is not a replacement for the original literature, but rather a tool to assist you in exploring and applying the concepts efficiently. Please utilize this worksheet in conjunction with the text to gain a full knowledge.

Guidelines for using the workbook:

- Chapter Summaries: Each chapter summary gives a succinct review of the main topics and ideas from that chapter. Use these summaries as a reminder or fast reference before beginning the workbook tasks.

- Primary Takeaways: After reading each chapter summary, make a note of the primary takeaways that connect with you. These thoughts might serve as a springboard for further thought and application in your own professional path.

- Self-Reflection Questions: Each chapter has a series of self-reflection questions intended to encourage contemplation about your work experiences and opinions. Take your time thinking about these questions, and consider writing your responses for clarity.

  Life-Changing Exercises: The workbook includes a range of exercises based on the teachings in What

Lights You Up?. These exercises aim to help you implement the book's themes while also encouraging personal growth, self-awareness, and empowerment. Choose workouts that you enjoy and incorporate them into your daily routine to get long-term results.

- Self-Evaluation Questions: At the end of the workbook, you'll discover self-evaluation questions to help you monitor your success and improvement as you map out your professional path. Use these questions to evaluate your accomplishments, identify areas for growth, and create goals for your future development.

OVERVIEW

Mary Olson-Menzel's What Lights You Up?: Illuminate Your Path and Take the Next Big Step in Your Career is a practical handbook for those looking to identify and pursue occupations that match their passions and beliefs. Whether readers are seasoned professionals searching for a career change, stay-at-home parents re-entering the industry, or recent graduates eager to get started, this book provides step-by-step tactics for achieving professional success.

Olson-Menzel's MVP 360 Coaching program provides a combination of personal development exercises and professional coaching. Readers are invited to consider their individual talents and "light"—the innate passions that motivate and guide them to achievement. The book focuses on crucial topics such as self-awareness, storytelling, and personal branding to assist readers in crafting their professional narrative and effectively presenting oneself in today's employment market. The author underlines the necessity of developing a personal brand to attract employers using technologies such as LinkedIn and social media.

Olson-Menzel not only helps readers identify their professional identity, but she also gives thorough advice on how to succeed in job interviews and negotiations. She explains how to approach networking with goal and purpose, create a supportive group, and stay positive throughout the job search process. The book also emphasizes the significance of developing long-term professional goals while being adaptable enough to capitalize on unforeseen chances.

Olson-Menzel's advice does not end with job hunting; she also provides readers with advice on how to continue their professional progression once they have a job. She emphasizes that the first three months of a new job are crucial for developing relationships, understanding organizational dynamics, and laying the groundwork for long-term success. Readers are urged to take control of their own growth, keep investing in their abilities, and establish habits that promote well-being and balance throughout their careers.

What lights you up? blends real-life success stories with practical advice, resulting in not just an educational career guide but also a motivating call to action for individuals looking for meaning and joy in their job. Olson-Menzel provides readers with the tools they need to survive in the ever-changing workplace by emphasizing personal values, purposeful decision-making, and long-term success.

CHAPTER 1: IDENTIFY YOUR LIGHT

Chapter Summary:

This chapter focuses on self-awareness as the cornerstone for work contentment. Olson-Menzel encourages readers to focus on their interests, abilities, and beliefs to discover what genuinely motivates them. Readers gain clarity on the type of work that will provide them with long-term fulfillment by examining previous successes and joys. The chapter promotes deep reflection to uncover what "lights you up" and distinguishes you in the professional world.

Key Takeaways:

- Self-awareness is the first step in having a fulfilling career.

- Your abilities, passions, and ideals are all unique to you.

- Reflecting on prior happy memories exposes your primary motivators.

- Clarity on what motivates you is vital for work happiness.

- Understanding your "light" helps you choose the appropriate route.

- Career fulfillment comes from combining job and passion.

- Introspection is essential in determining your genuine purpose.

- Knowing your light enables a more concentrated job hunt.

Self-Reflection Questions:

Which activities make you feel the most alive and energized?

_____

_____

_____

_____

_____

When have you been completely fulfilled in your professional or personal life?

_____

_____

_____

_____

_____

How do your personal values relate to your professional goals?

_____

_____

_____

_____

_____

_____

_____

What strengths have people regularly identified in you?

_____

_____

_____

_____

_____

_____

_____

How would you define success for yourself?

_____

_____

_____

_____

_____

_____

What patterns emerge when you think on your fondest moments?

_____

_____

_____

_____

_____

_____

Life-Changing Exercises:

Create a list of activities that make you feel energized and happy.

Consider three previous professional or personal triumphs and examine what made them gratifying.

Make a mental map outlining your abilities, interests, and values.

Keep a daily log of the times you felt particularly interested or thrilled.

Identify a role model that exhibits a job that inspires you and research their path.

Create a vision board for your dream career and lifestyle.

Ask three close friends or coworkers to identify your strongest abilities.

Make a list of non-negotiable values you desire in your job.

Discover a new activity or talent that interests you and matches with your passions.

Set aside one hour every week to focus on your developing sense of purpose.

Would you like to proceed with the remaining chapters in a similar manner?

CHAPTER 2: TURN THE LIGHT ON

Chapter Summary:

This chapter focuses on engaging your interests and taking the initial actions toward making your goals come true. Olson-Menzel highlights the necessity of transitioning from self-awareness to action through tiny but substantial stages. She urges readers to embrace their passions and use their newfound clarity to their everyday lives and careers. The chapter emphasizes the need of confidence, tenacity, and perseverance in translating ideas into concrete results.

Key Takeaways:

- Self-awareness must result in action.
- Taking modest steps increases momentum.
- When it comes to following your dreams, you must have courage.
- Begin adding passion into your regular activities.
- Confidence is built via regular action.

- Persistence is essential in conquering problems.

- It's critical to prioritize what motivates you.

- Action turns insight into actual results.

Self-Reflection Questions:

What is one simple move I can take today to achieve my goals?

_____

_____

_____

_____

_____

_____

How does fear keep me from taking action?

_____

_____

_____

_____

_____

_____

What is one way I can incorporate my interest into my existing lifestyle?

_____

_____

_____

_____

_____

_____

How can I gain confidence in areas where I am uncertain?

_____

_____

_____

_____

_____

_____

What prevented me from chasing my aspirations in the past?

_____

_____

_____

_____

_____

_____

How can I remember myself to continue in the face of setbacks?

_____

_____

_____

_____

_____

_____

_____

Life-Changing Exercises:

Set a daily goal to work on your interest, even if it's just for 10 minutes.

Break down a huge professional objective into smaller, more doable activities.

Every week, set a challenge for yourself to accomplish something scary.

Create an accountability partner with whom you can discuss your progress.

Practice affirmations that can boost your bravery and confidence.

Create a "success jar" in which you record your daily successes, large or little.

Identify one habit that interferes with your attention and make a commitment to replace it.

Volunteer in an area similar to your passion.

Schedule weekly reflection sessions to assess your progress and future moves.

Create a customized motto to help you stay focused on your light.

CHAPTER 3: WRITE YOUR STORY.

Chapter Summary:

In this chapter, Olson-Menzel urges readers to create their own personal and professional narratives. Individuals who precisely articulate their narrative may express their abilities, beliefs, and ambitions to potential employers and networks more effectively. The chapter emphasizes the necessity of taking ownership of your path, including both accomplishments and problems, and using these experiences to form your professional identity. Writing your narrative helps to clarify your work goals and allows you to convey yourself genuinely and forcefully.

Key Takeaways:

- Your narrative determines your professional identity.
- Articulating your story allows you to stand out.
- Each encounter adds to your adventure.

- Authenticity is essential while telling your tale.

- Take responsibility for your accomplishments as well as your shortcomings.

- Your tale should be about your beliefs and ambitions.

- Your story must be consistent with your career goals.

- Telling your narrative effectively increases your professional influence.

Self-Reflection Questions:

How does my tale convey my essential values?

_____

_____

_____

_____

_____

_____

What obstacles have influenced me, and how have I evolved as a result?

_____

_____

_____

_____

_____

What strengths have resulted from my unique experiences?

_____

_____

_____

_____

_____

_____

How can I communicate my experience in a way that connects with others?

_____

_____

_____

_____

_____

_____

What is the common thread in my personal and professional lives?

_____

_____

_____

_____

_____

_____

How does my story relate to my future job goals?

_____

_____

_____

_____

_____

_____

Life-Changing Exercises:

Create a timeline of your life, emphasizing important milestones.

Identify a problem you overcame and how it influenced your professional identity.

Develop a personal mission statement that matches your essential principles.

Create a professional bio for your LinkedIn profile that summarizes your story.

Try discussing your tale with a trustworthy friend or mentor.

Create a list of "defining moments" in your career.

Reframe a previous failure as a learning opportunity in your narrative.

Compare your present CV to the tale you wish to convey; what needs to change?

Create an elevator pitch that tells your story in under 60 seconds.

Consider how your narrative might inspire people in your profession.

Do you want me to continue with the following chapters?

CHAPTER 4: BUILDING YOUR TOOLBOX

Chapter Summary:

This chapter emphasizes the necessity of having a varied mix of skills and tools to successfully navigate the employment market. Olson-Menzel urges readers to evaluate their present abilities, identify gaps, and look for possibilities to improve. She offers practical ways for developing a "toolbox" of hard and soft skills, certifications, and experiences that correspond with professional goals. The chapter highlights lifelong learning and adaptation as critical components of success in any industry.

Key Takeaways:

- A diversified skill set increases your marketability.
- Determine where your existing talents fall short of your professional objectives.

- Seek for possibilities for ongoing learning to advance your career.

- Both hard and soft talents are critical for success.

- Certifications might help you establish reputation in your area.

- Real-life experiences supplement conventional education.

- Networking might provide up chances for skill improvement.

- Adaptability is vital in today's continuously changing labor market.

Self-Reflection Questions:

What talents do I presently possess that are relevant to my professional goals?

_____

_____

_____

_____

_____

_____

Which abilities do I need to improve in order to grow in my field?

_____

_____

_____

_____

_____

_____

How have my previous experiences influenced my present
skill set?

_____

_____

_____

_____

_____

_____

What resources can I use to develop new skills?

_____

_____

_____

_____

_____

_____

How can I use my existing abilities in new ways?

_____

_____

_____

_____

_____

_____

What learning chances have I missed in the past?

_____

_____

_____

_____

_____

_____

Life-Changing Exercises:

Create a skills inventory by identifying all of your existing talents.

Identify three talents you wish to master and create a strategy to achieve them.

Find and enroll in an online course that is relevant to your job aspirations.

Join a professional association that provides workshop and networking opportunities.

Seek for a mentor who can assist you find talents to improve.

Volunteer for projects at work that require you to learn new skills.

Attend industry conferences and webinars to broaden your expertise.

Start a blog or portfolio to showcase your talents and projects.

Participate in local community activities to enhance soft skills such as communication.

Set aside time each week for self-directed study or skill development.

CHAPTER 5: FOLLOW YOUR DREAM.

Chapter Summary:

This chapter inspires readers to follow their ambitions with dedication and enthusiasm. Olson-Menzel emphasizes the need of connecting professional choices with personal goals and beliefs. She offers ways for overcoming worries and self-doubt, which are common when pursuing one's aspirations. The chapter highlights the value of visualization and goal-setting as tools for motivating and focusing individuals on their desired results.

Key Takeaways:

- Pursuing your aspirations demands focus and dedication.
- Align your job decisions with your personal beliefs.
- Overcoming fear is vital for pursuing your ambitions.
- Visualization can help you achieve your goals.

- Setting specific goals helps you stay accountable and focused.

- Celebrate tiny victories along the way to stay motivated.

- Developing a growth mentality increases your resilience.

- Seeking encouragement from others can help your efforts.

Self-Reflection Questions:

What is my deepest dream, and how does it fit with my values?

_____

_____

_____

_____

_____

_____

What worries are preventing me from pursuing my dreams?

_____

_____

_____

_____

_____

_____

How can I picture my success and inspire myself?

_____

_____

_____

_____

_____

_____

What particular goals can I make to go closer to my dream?

_____

_____

_____

_____

_____

_____

How have I overcome hurdles in the past to reach my goals?

_____

_____

_____

_____

_____

_____

Who can I turn to for help and encouragement on my journey?

_____

_____

_____

_____

_____

_____

_____

Life-Changing Exercises:

Write a letter to your future self, telling how you fulfilled your dream.

Create a vision board to symbolize your ambitions and goals.

Break down your desire into specific, time-bound targets.

Create a mantra to remind yourself of your dedication to your ambitions.

Find motivation by researching people who have attained comparable goals.

Set up monthly check-ins to evaluate your progress toward your goals.

Create a thankfulness diary to appreciate your journey and tiny successes.

To ensure accountability, share your dreams with a trustworthy friend or mentor.

Make a plan to overcome possible roadblocks in your way.

Set aside time each week to take actions toward your ambition, no matter how modest.

CHAPTER 6: TAP INTO YOUR NETWORK

Chapter Summary:

This chapter discusses the value of networking in accomplishing career objectives. Olson-Menzel highlights the importance of developing and sustaining relationships in order to have access to opportunities and resources. She provides tips for effective networking, such as how to approach new contacts and nurture current ones. The chapter urges readers to use their networks for support, mentorship, and cooperation as they achieve their professional goals.

Key Takeaways:

- Networking is vital for job advancement and opportunities.
- Developing real relationships is more beneficial than transactional networking.

- Approach new relationships with sincerity and openness.

- Nurturing existing connections might result in unexpected possibilities.

- Seek mentors who can offer direction and assistance.

- Networking may help you expand your knowledge and skill set.

- Collaboration may open doors and generate new opportunities.

- A diversified network provides different viewpoints and resources.

Self-Reflection Questions:

How have my previous networking encounters affected my career?

_____

_____

_____

_____

_____

Who in my present network can help me achieve my professional goals?

_____

_____

_____

_____

_____

What are my talents in networking, and where can I improve?

_____

_____

_____

_____

_____

_____

How can I help my network grow and strengthen relationships?

_____

_____

_____

_____

_____

_____

What are my objectives for growing my professional network?

_____

_____

_____

_____

_____

_____

How do I feel when I contact new individuals about networking opportunities?

_____

_____

_____

_____

_____

_____

Life-Changing Exercises:

Attend local networking events to meet new people in your industry.

Contact an old coworker to catch up and reconnect.

Schedule monthly coffee talks with people in your business.

Join online professional organizations or forums relevant to your profession.

Create a list of people you admire and contact them for informative interviews.

Volunteer with professional groups to increase your network.

Use LinkedIn to connect with others and share useful information.

Offer to help someone in your network attain their objectives.

Practice your elevator pitch for networking opportunities.

Maintain a networking log to track contacts and follow-ups.

CHAPTER 7: CHOOSE JOY.

Chapter Summary:

This chapter emphasizes the importance of generating joy in one's professional journey. Olson-Menzel contends that a happy perspective boosts resilience and inventiveness, allowing people to overcome problems more efficiently. The chapter discusses techniques for incorporating pleasure into daily professional life, stressing gratitude and mindfulness as vital practices. By concentrating on what makes them happy, readers are encouraged to have a more rewarding and enjoyable work experience.

Key Takeaways:

- Choosing pleasure improves your thinking and productivity.

- A thankfulness habit may change your outlook.

- Mindfulness helps you stay present and relieves stress.

- Focus on tasks and settings that make you happy.

- Surrounding oneself with favorable influences improves morale.

- Accepting problems as opportunities brings delight.

- Celebrate your accomplishments, no matter how minor.

- Joyful situations can boost creativity and inventiveness.

Self-Reflection Questions:

What employment activities provide me the greatest joy?

_____

_____

_____

_____

_____

How can I work more thankfulness into my everyday routine?

_____

_____

_____

_____

_____

_____

What negative influences may I reduce to increase my joy?

_____

_____

_____

_____

_____

_____

How do I respond to problems, and can I change my perspective?

_____

_____

_____

_____

_____

_____

What modest accomplishments can I celebrate this week?

_____

_____

_____

_____

_____

_____

How can I foster a positive work environment for myself and others?

_____

_____

_____

_____

_____

_____

Life-Changing Exercises:

Begin each day by naming three things you're grateful for.

Incorporate thoughtful techniques, such as meditation, into your daily routine.

Set aside time each week to indulge in a pleasurable activity.

Make a pleasure notebook to record pleasant occurrences.

Identify and eliminate one harmful influence from your professional life.

Plan a little celebration to mark a recent accomplishment.

Set aside time to focus on happy experiences from your week.

Recognize coworkers' accomplishments to spread delight among them.

Discover new activities outside of work that make you happy.

Challenge yourself to find joy in a challenging work or circumstance.

CHAPTER 8: DEVELOPING YOUR THREE PS

Chapter Summary:

Chapter Summary: In this chapter, Olson-Menzel presents the "Three Ps": Passion, Purpose, and Persistence. She demonstrates how these three factors are essential for establishing a successful and rewarding job. Readers may develop a long-term professional path that aligns with their basic beliefs and objectives by discovering personal passions, linking them with a sense of purpose, and persevering in the face of challenges.

Key Takeaways:

- Passion fosters motivation and engagement at work.

- Your career gains focus and significance when you have a clear purpose.

- Persistence is essential for overcoming challenges and disappointments.

- Aligning interests and purpose improves job happiness.

- Reflecting on your values helps you define your work objectives.

- Developing resilience improves your capacity to deal with adversity.

- Celebrating progress encourages a sense of success.

- Continuous self-assessment helps you stay on track with your goals.

Self-Reflection Questions:

What am I actually enthusiastic about in my career?

_____

_____

_____

_____

_____

_____

How does my employment fit into my sense of purpose?

_____

_____

_____

_____

_____

_____

In what areas do I need to be more persistent?

_____

_____

_____

_____

_____

_____

What values are most important to me at work?

_____

_____

_____

_____

_____

_____

How can I track my progress toward my goals?

_____

_____

_____

_____

_____

_____

What recent trials have I conquered, and what lessons have

I learned?

_____

_____

_____

_____

_____

_____

Life-Changing Exercises:

List your top three passions and how they connect to your career.

Create a mission statement that represents your professional goals.

Set short- and long-term objectives that are in line with your interests and purpose.

Keep a diary to record your challenges and answers to them.

Every month, review your progress and change your goals as needed.

Engage in activities that promote perseverance, such as a tough project.

Seek input from mentors to determine areas for development.

Investigate volunteer options that correspond with your interests.

Attend classes or activities that will spark your passion and purpose.

Create a strategy for retaining persistence during difficult circumstances.

CHAPTER 9: SHINE IN THE INTERVIEW AND LAND THE JOB.

Chapter Summary:

This chapter focuses on the most important parts of job interviews and landing a position. Olson-Menzel offers practical advice on how to prepare for interviews, present oneself successfully, and communicate value to prospective employers. She highlights the value of narrative and authenticity in interviews, urging readers to boldly share their unique experiences and abilities.

Key Takeaways:

- A good interview requires thorough preparation.

- Practice popular interview questions to increase your confidence.

- Authenticity establishes a true relationship with interviewees.

- Storytelling is a great way to express your experiences.

- Research the firm to ensure your replies are consistent with its ideals.

- Body language is extremely important in initial impressions.

- Ask intelligent questions to show your interest.

- Follow-up communication confirms your excitement for the position.

Self-Reflection Questions:

What talents and experiences would I like to highlight during an interview?

_____

_____

_____

_____

_____

How can I properly share my story with potential employers?

_____

_____

_____

_____

_____

_____

What frequent interview questions should I prepare for?

_____

_____

_____

_____

_____

_____

How do I generally portray myself during interviews?

_____

_____

_____

_____

_____

_____

_____

What research should I undertake on possible employers?

_____

_____

_____

_____

_____

_____

How do I deal with anxieties during interviews, and how can I improve?

_____

_____

_____

_____

_____

_____

Life-Changing Exercises:

Practice by doing mock interviews with friends or mentors.

Create and practice your personal story as it pertains to your career.

Make a list of probable interview questions and rehearse your answers.

Research three firms you admire and prepare specific questions for each.

Record yourself during practice interviews to evaluate your body language and tone.

Reflect on previous interview experiences and identify lessons learnt.

Create a follow-up thank-you message template to use after interviews.

Create a portfolio that highlights your accomplishments and talents.

Network with specialists in your sector to get knowledge on interview tactics.

Set explicit objectives for each interview, such as decreasing nervousness or improving replies.

Do you want to continue with the future chapters?

CHAPTER 10: SUCCEED TODAY.

Chapter Summary:

Chapter Summary: In this chapter, Olson-Menzel highlights the need of adopting quick, practical efforts to attain professional success. She urges readers to focus on everyday behaviors that lead to long-term success, emphasizing the importance of minor victories and constant work. The chapter offers practical advice for retaining motivation and accountability, as well as ideas for responding to changing working conditions.

Key Takeaways:

- Taking little, consistent activities results in substantial growth.

- Daily practices influence your long-term performance.

- Celebrating little victories increases motivation and morale.

- Establishing a routine increases productivity and attention.

- Being adaptive allows you to handle workplace changes.

- Accountability partners can help you stay committed.

- Prioritizing activities based on importance improves effectiveness.

- Self-reflection is necessary for continued progress.

Self-Reflection Questions:

What little steps can I take today to go closer to my goal?

_____

_____

_____

_____

_____

_____

How do my everyday behaviors impact my overall success?

_____

_____

_____

_____

_____

_____

What recent achievements may I celebrate?

_____

_____

_____

_____

_____

_____

_____

How adaptive am I in the face of change?

_____

_____

_____

_____

_____

_____

_____

Who can I turn to for responsibility in my career?

_____

_____

_____

_____

_____

_____

What priorities should I reconsider to increase my effectiveness?

_____

_____

_____

_____

_____

_____

Life-Changing Exercises:

Make a daily action plan with specific activities that are linked with your goals.

Consider your everyday behaviors and discover places for improvement.

List three recent successes and congratulate them.

Create a morning ritual to establish a positive tone for the day.

Seek out an accountability buddy to discuss objectives and progress.

Prioritize your chores each week using the Eisenhower Matrix.

Set aside time each week for self-reflection on your professional path.

Schedule time for skill improvement to improve your professional possibilities.

Monitor your progress and revise your action plan as appropriate.

End each day by identifying three accomplishments.

CHAPTER 11: CREATE FORWARD MOMENTUM.

Chapter Summary:

This chapter discusses the necessity of keeping momentum in one's profession. Olson-Menzel explains ways to overcome stagnation and promote ongoing progress. She highlights the need of establishing new objectives, receiving feedback, and embracing lifelong learning as methods to stay motivated and avoid complacency in one's work life.

Key Takeaways:

- Continuous progress necessitates establishing new and difficult goals.

- Seeking feedback is critical to personal and professional growth.

- Lifelong learning keeps skills current and increases flexibility.

- A growth mentality promotes resilience and optimism.

- Reflecting on prior experiences might help you find possibilities for growth.

- Networking brings up new opportunities and insights.

- Embracing change can lead to unforeseen growth opportunities.

- Celebrating progress strengthens motivation and commitment.

Self-Reflection Questions:

What additional goals can I establish to push myself further?

_____

_____

_____

_____

_____

_____

How frequently do I seek input from others?

_____

_____

_____

_____

_____

_____

What skills should I develop to remain relevant in my field?

_____

_____

_____

_____

_____

_____

How can I develop a development attitude in my everyday work?

_____

_____

_____

_____

_____

_____

_____

What prior experiences can help shape my future growth?

_____

_____

_____

_____

_____

_____

How can I broaden my network to generate new opportunities?

_____

_____

_____

_____

_____

_____

Life-Changing Exercises:

Set a new professional objective for the next six months and plan how to attain it.

Seek and act on constructive input from coworkers or mentors.

Enroll in a course or workshop to learn new skills.

Reflect on your job path and identify critical learning experiences.

Attend networking events to make new professional contacts.

Make a vision board to imagine your future objectives and dreams.

Set up regular check-ins with yourself to measure your progress.

Start a book club dedicated to personal and professional growth.

Join a professional association relevant to your field.

Commit to learning something new every month.

CHAPTER 12: DEVELOP A FRAMEWORK FOR SUCCESS

Chapter Summary:

Olson-Menzel's last chapter lays forth a complete framework for attaining long-term professional success. She highlights the need of combining the ideas presented throughout the book into a cohesive plan. The chapter invites readers to construct a personal roadmap that includes their interests, beliefs, and aspirations, ensuring that their professional trajectory remains true to their real self.

Key Takeaways:

- A defined framework directs your professional decisions and actions.
- Integrating passions and values results in greater fulfillment.

- Regularly reviewing your goals keeps you on track with your vision.

- Flexibility is required when modifying the framework to new situations.

- A personal roadmap serves as a compass for professional decisions.

- Collaboration and support networks improve your trip.

- Self-assessment allows you to fine-tune your goals and techniques.

- Celebrating achievements boosts motivation and promotes commitment.

Self-Reflection Questions:

What components should my personal framework for success include?

_____

_____

_____

_____

_____

How do my hobbies and values impact my professional choices?

_____

_____

_____

_____

_____

How frequently do I revisit and revise my professional goals?

_____

_____

_____

_____

_____

_____

What hurdles can I face while putting my framework into action?

_____

_____

_____

_____

_____

_____

Who can help me create and manage my success framework?

_____

_____

_____

_____

_____

_____

How will I commemorate the milestones on my journey?

_____

_____

_____

_____

_____

_____

Life-Changing Exercises:

Create a personal success framework that includes your objectives, values, and interests.

Create a five-year plan outlining your career goals.

To ensure that your framework remains aligned with your goals, revisit and change it quarterly.

Get input from trustworthy peers on your framework and goals.

Create a support network of peers who can hold you accountable.

Create a set of milestones to track your progress.

Use visualization approaches to strengthen your framework.

Attend career development workshops to help you enhance your framework.

Make a self-care strategy to promote your mental and emotional health.

Keep a journal of your experiences and framework revisions on a regular basis.

Please let me know if you need anything else!

SELF-EVALUATION QUESTIONS

What personal beliefs and interests drive my job decisions?

_____

_____

_____

_____

_____

_____

How do I define success in my work life?

_____

_____

_____

_____

_____

_____

_____

In what ways have I taken steps to achieve my job goals?

_____

_____

_____

_____

_____

_____

What skills or expertise do I now need to develop?

_____

_____

_____

_____

_____

_____

How successfully do I use my network to advance my career?

_____

_____

_____

_____

_____

_____

What fears or difficulties have I faced while following my dreams?

_____

_____

_____

_____

_____

_____

_____

How can I commemorate my accomplishments and milestones?

_____

_____

_____

_____

_____

_____

What input did I get, and how did I use it?

_____

_____

_____

_____

_____

_____

_____

How adaptive am I when faced with setbacks in my career?

_____

_____

_____

_____

_____

_____

What daily routines are beneficial to my professional development?

_____

_____

_____

_____

_____

_____

How successfully do I communicate my own narrative with others?

_____

_____

_____

_____

_____

_____

How can I keep my career moving forward?

_____

_____

_____

_____

_____

_____

_____

How can I handle stress while still enjoying my work?

_____

_____

_____

_____

_____

_____

How can I search for learning opportunities?

_____

_____

_____

_____

_____

_____

_____

How frequently do I evaluate and alter my work path to match with my goals?

_____

_____

_____

_____

_____

_____

_____

_____

_____

_____

_____

_____

_____

Made in the USA
Las Vegas, NV
02 November 2024

11037891R00063